THE HEALING POWER OF WORDS

Rev J Martin

ISBN-13: 978-1717492852
ISBN-10: 1717492851

DEDICATION

I dedicate this book to my family, for their constant love and support.

CONTENTS

ACKNOWLEDGMENTS

This book would not have been possible without the support and encouragement of my family, and the inspiration from my Heavenly Father.

A special thanks to my editor and all the people a Pixal Design Studios for the lovely design work, and Amazon for providing the digital tools by which I can get my message out into the world.

Finally, I would like to thank YOU, for buying my book, may it enlighten your life and bring you peace.

Introduction

When life is comfortable, everything seems easy. When life is difficult, everything seems hard. Why do we end up in these spirals of "all good" or "all bad"?

And, how can we get out of the "all bad" faster, next time we get trapped? How can we help ourselves get out of there?

It's all about learning The Healing Power Of Words.

Healing words can come in many different forms; you can say them, read them, or have them said to you. All are extremely powerful. This book will cover all three.

I've had periods in my life when all hope seemed lost. When just facing another day was a challenge. When I could see no way out of my current situation, or I convinced myself, what I was going through was my destiny.

My struggles have often led to physical illness, anxiety, stress, and depression, all affecting my body in strange ways.

We all deal with situations differently, but when things are against me, I pray more intensely, I read motivational books, I become more solitary. I look into methods to help me get out of my negative state.

If you are anything like me, the slightest little thing can knock you off-course. You're having an amazing day, and someone says something that annoys you, instantly changing your mood, which results in you speaking or acting in a way that is entirely out of character.

It could even be someone cutting in front of you on the motorway. They are 100% in the wrong, but you let their actions affect you for the rest of the day. You keep replaying the dialogue in your head, over and over. "I just can't believe they cut in front of me."

Our mind has the habit of getting stuck on repeat. The same thought looping over and over; let it out. Grab a pen and paper or sit down in front of your computer and write. Doing this clears your mind, allowing you to think more clearly.

"This too will pass," is my favorite quote. These words help me greatly when I'm going through something I think will never change. No matter what you are going through at this moment, it will change. It might not completely change tomorrow, but it will be different, if ever just slightly.

Words have the power to help you see the world from a different perspective. Words have the power to strengthen bonds that are falling apart. Words have the power to heal you and those around you.

The words in this book can heal your life.

Home Sweet Home

The first place to start using healing words is with your family. How long has it been since you told the people in your life, “I love you, you're gifted, you're talented, and you will achieve great things.” How long has it been since you spoke those words over your own life?

Many people can’t speak healing words because they don’t have any healing words to say about themselves. We can beat ourselves up every day, thinking of our faults, listing all the reasons we don’t measure up.

We’re not as attractive as we would like or as popular. We don’t have the car or a house like our friends. This negativity can affect our spirit, so much so we can take it out on the people closest to us with sharp, hurtful comments.

What can happen is, you can neglect your husband or wife, and then a stranger compliments him or her a few times a week. They come home on a high, which quickly evaporates. If you're not careful, you can push away the very people you love and care about.

Every time you tell your wife she's beautiful, she shines a little brighter. Every time you say to your husband, thanks for the support, he feels valued. Not only are they getting stronger, but the marriage is also getting stronger.

The same can happen with your children. You can be so wrapped up in your own life that you fail to encourage them, comfort them, and make them feel accepted for who they are.

Children crave attention, encouragement, and acceptance. If they don't get it from their parents, then they will get it from someone else, their teacher, their coach or the gang on the other side of town.

Every day, speak faith and blessings over the people in your life with your words. Let them know what they mean to you, let them know that you care, let them know what they can achieve.

Be the water they need to grow, be the sunshine they need to bloom, be the wind that propels them forward into their destiny. Remind them they are full of potential and they have been perfectly made. God is by their side, watching and protecting them. Taking the wisdom of the past, you can stand on the shoulders of giants; you can grow spiritually.

There is so much to deal with these days. Saying hurtful and belittling things is almost looked at as a form of amusement. Being on the wrong side of bullying in my younger and adult life, I can tell you from first-hand experience. It is far from amusing.

Parents often say to me, why did my son never speak of bullying? Why did he never say he felt intimidated? Why did he not let me know?

It's important to speak positivity over your children, friends, and co-workers on a daily basis. You have no idea what is going on in their lives. Now, with social media, a person doesn't even have to be in your presence. They can say hurtful things to you 24 hours a day.

Now more than ever, we all need positive words, words of faith and encouragement, spoken over our lives to drown out the negativity.

When you tell your children, "I love you, you're highly talented, and I know you will achieve great things in your life," those words are doing more than you can imagine. They create a force field that surrounds them wherever they go.

Hurtful words will not have the same impact, as they know deep within that those words are coming from a place of negativity.

Always speak positive, faithful healing words.

Day Of Judgment

Matthew 12:36

And I tell you this; you must give an account on judgment day for every idle word you speak.

Idle words mean negative, hurtful words. When God comes to answer your prayers, He will say, how are you treating the family, friends, and neighbors I gave you? Are you helping them grow, are you treating them with respect? Are you helping them to become more confident and more secure?

If the people in your life are not growing, evolving, developing into stronger, more confident, faithful people, you need to ask yourself, "Am I speaking healing or hurtful words?"

Is your family, your friends, and your co-workers better today than they were five years ago? Are they stronger, happier, and more fulfilled?

If not, then you need to make some changes.

God gave them to you; He's expecting you to nourish them with healing words, to strengthen, motivate and encourage them, to fulfill what He put in their hearts.

When some peoples' Day of Judgment comes, it will be a sad day. When God looks at their life, all He will see is pain, heartache, and suffering, families torn apart from betrayal, stubbornness, bitterness, and anger. Don't let that be you.

Use your words to heal people. Use your words to build them up by strengthening, encouraging, and motivating them. Use your words to instill faith in their hearts.

Mend What's Broken

Seamus was a successful lawyer, a very wealthy self-made man who had a beautiful home, a loving wife, and three children. Anyone looking at his life would have thought he had everything. The truth, Seamus life was crumbling. His wife of 10 years was filing for a divorce.

He agreed with all her reasons. He was always at the office doing overtime, and when he was home, he was planning for the next case, never making time for her or his children. His job had completely taken over his life.

Seamus had lost sight of what mattered.

Since being kicked out of the house, he had only argued with his wife, which made the situation worse. Many nasty, hurtful things were said. Now, she wouldn't even answer his calls. "What can I do to save my marriage?" he asked, in a way that he expected me to have the answer. I thought of Proverbs 15:4, Kind words heal and help; cutting words wound and maim. So I suggested taking a step back to let tempers calm.

Often, when calm healing words are needed is when people give into their emotions and make things worse.

I advised him that, for his wife to change her mind, she first would have to feel that he had changed, his words and actions reflecting this change. He said he would do whatever I suggested, so in silent prayer, I prayed for an answer to reveal itself.

The idea that came to mind was for him to write a letter to his wife and, in that letter, admit his actions were wrong and ask for forgiveness. List all the reasons why he would miss her and the children. Tell her what he admired about her, what he loved about her, what he respected about her. On leaving, he looked upbeat.

When we get no encouragement, no compliments, no love from a person, we can slowly drift apart. Then on top of that, if there are hurtful or damaging words spoken, relationship bonds can be broken.

To heal relationships, loving, caring and compassionate words are needed, not hurtful, damaging, and destructive ones.

Before a relationship breaks down, there will be many warning signs; do not dismiss them. I'm sure Seamus's wife told him repeatedly that she was unhappy. I'm sure his children longed for a dad that played with them or took them on adventures.

In the busyness of life, we all can miss out on what really matters. We all can easily neglect the simple things that give our life purpose.

A few months later, Seamus and his wife approached me, very emotional, telling me how my advice had saved their marriage and asking how they could ever repay me.

I just asked them to keep compliments the main part of their family life and encourage each other. Let their children know there are great things in their futures. Push them on. Never tell them they can't do anything. Fuel their creativity, fuel their passions, and fuel their love for life.

I'm Busy, Do not Disturb

Lift your head, put the phone away; nothing is more rewarding than helping someone else rise higher. When we look back on our lives, we can be known for a lot of things, a person of great faith, a person of integrity, a person of great material wealth, and that is all good.

But I would rather be known for inspiring people, for motivating people, for turning people's flame of faith into a raging fire, a fire that burns all negativity from their lives.

There are enough people saying hurtful, negative, and judgmental words. Our attitude should be, "Who can I help today, who can I inspire, who can I motivate to reach higher, go further, dream bigger?"

Instilling faith in others instills faith in you.

When you begin to see the power you possess simply by speaking words over your life and the lives of others, you begin to realize how almighty God Himself spoke worlds into existence.

When Jesus said, you will do similar works, and greater works than me –John 14:12, this is what He meant. Words have the power to turn someone's life upside down. Words can save a marriage, rebuild a friendship, make you believe in yourself again.

See how these words make you feel. "I'm tired, I'm lonely, I'm depressed." Now see how different these words make you feel. "My energy flows from God, I will be the friend I want to have, I may feel low now, but I know there are brighter days ahead."

Who will your words inspire? Start with the reflection in the mirror.

Self Love

Healing, health, and happiness all come from the same source. Love. If you're in a place today where you don't love yourself, it's hard to become someone who does. Self-love takes practice. Self-love is not selfish; it means you value who you are. A child of God, made perfect in every way.

One method of self-love is to allow love to flow through you as often as possible. Focus on how you can encourage, motivate, and help the people in your life.

It's easy to be loving towards ourselves when things are going as planned, when we succeed, and people like us. It's when things fall apart, or we get rejected that we struggle the most. That's when we tend to be hardest on ourselves.

In those moments, ask yourself how someone who loved you would treat you. What would they do? What would they say? How would they behave? Chances are, they wouldn't judge, criticise, or belittle you. They'd offer you acceptance, kindness, and compassion. They would say things like: you're intelligent, you're beautiful, it's fun spending time with you.

Life is hard enough without running ourselves down. Stop comparing your life to someone else's. No matter how well you know him or her, you never know how he or she feels or how they perceive their life.

You would think everyone that lived in the Hollywood Hills would be happy, but they're not. Many have deep depression and depend on drugs to get them through the day. Does that sound like a dream life?

Start spending your time and energy nourishing and encouraging yourself. Take action— turn those dreams into reality. Honor and care for yourself.

By praying daily and speaking words of faith, you are signaling that you're worthy of living the life you desire. It doesn't have to be significant action. Small and consistent steps in the direction that stirs joy, care, and love will do.

When you feel good about yourself, it means your thinking is aligned with how God sees you. When you feel bad about yourself, it's a red flag telling you that your connection to God is broken. You need a fresh perspective.

If you think a thought such as "I am overweight." How does that feel? Probably not that good. That's a sign to think a different thought. Try to replace that with something kinder. For example, "I am going to walk each day, so I'm fit and healthy."

Start caring for yourself. Create habits that are healthy, not only mentally, but also emotionally.

Do this, and you will not believe the difference it will make.

Healing the Body and Mind

Proverbs 4:20-22

"My son, pay attention to what I say; turn your ear to my words. Do not let them out of your sight, keep them within your heart; for they are life to those who find them and health to one's whole body."

Reading scripture can have a powerful healing effect on both body and mind. We can easily drift away from God with the stresses of life. Doubts and worries can get too much; we must consciously speak healing, encouraging words over our lives.

When we listen to news, radio, or spend time on social media, it's easy to let negative words corrode our spirit. The gossip, slander, and rumors can seem like fun, as long as you are not the one people are talking about.

These kinds of words are what most workplaces thrive on. It's almost like you cannot fit in unless you are running somebody else down.

In the beginning, you may think you will rise above it, but stay in that environment long enough, and you will start to do the same. As the saying goes, "Birds of a feather flock together."

I always felt out of place in these sorts of environments. Initially, I put myself down for not being able to fit in, but as I got older and wiser, I realized I needed to be surrounded by different people.

People that showed compassion, people that showed empathy, people that showed a caring nature towards others.

As long as you remain around those that run others down, you will never grow into the person you were sent here to become. Plus, when you focus on the faults of others you will begin to see the faults in yourself.

Surround yourself with positive people, people of faith, people that want the best for you. Read scriptures each day to focus your mind on what really matters, our relationship with God. It will help you to de-stress, bringing positivity to your day, which will bring out the best in you.

Negative Self-Talk

I recall a night years ago, when I finally recognized how much I had been hurting myself with my persistent negative self-talk. I used to believe I wasn't talented enough, I wasn't spiritual enough, I wasn't good enough to fulfill my potential.

That night, I realized how damaging my negative self-talk had been, physically and spiritually. Upon this awareness, I burst into tears and cried.

I remembered all the times I had thought and believed negative thoughts about myself, saying things like, there's no point trying that; just keep quiet no one wants to hear your view. Don't do that; you'll only embarrass yourself. I began writing down all these thoughts. Reading the list, I knew something had to change.

The first step was forgiving myself for all the guilt and pain I had created in my life by repeatedly telling myself I wasn't good enough. Then I decided to take responsibility for my feelings and put an end to my suffering.

Much of the pain we experience is self-created through our words, thoughts, and beliefs about our circumstances. When we accept responsibility for our actions, we learn we have more control over our lives than we thought.

We can't control what happens to us, but we can choose how we let it affect us. Forgiving ourselves is a great starting point.

From here, you can choose to do things differently. Becoming aware of the thoughts you think and the words you speak about yourself.

It's so easy to focus on our weaknesses, speaking and thinking negative thoughts about ourselves. We need to make a conscious effort to focus on the positives in our lives.

I can, I will, I must.

Proverbs 4:23 (GNT)
Be careful how you think; your life is shaped by your thoughts.

Most Powerful Healing Words

When I was younger, every time I took my brother's toy or called my brother names, my mother would ask me to apologize.

An apology became my primary reaction to any mistake. At that time, I didn't understand the healing the words, "I am sorry," contained, but now I do.

It took me a long time to realize that those words needed to come from the heart. Apologizing just for the sake of it is meaningless if we can't admit to ourselves that we made a mistake. Placing the blame on someone else and making excuses is easy. Accepting the full weight of responsibility, however, is very hard.

Growing up, my best friend and I started becoming more competitive, and it went too far, ending up in an argument. We both refused to apologize because neither of us wanted to "give in."

Our stubbornness broke our friendship. If my wiser self could go back, I would have taken responsibility and resolved the problem. That simple action would have saved our friendship. Instead, I let my pride take priority.

Many people see apologizing as a sign of weakness, but for me, it is a sign of strength. Learning to apologize is the most crucial step in the healing process. Not only does it show the person that you acknowledge their right to feel hurt, but it opens the way to forgiveness.

How can two words be so powerful?

When we receive an apology, we feel the person that hurt us recognizes our pain and is willing to help us heal. "I'm sorry," cannot undo the action, but it can help ease the pain caused. It gives hope for regrowth and puts a value on the relationship, rather than the individual's pride.

The two simple words, "I'm sorry," are worth more than a lifetime of excuses and explanations.

Choose love above pride. Choose to apologize. Choose the path of healing.

Mark 11:35
And when you stand praying, if you hold anything against anyone, forgive them, so that your Father in heaven may forgive you your sins."

Three Words Can Save A Life

At college, I worked with a guy named Philip. We had a good working relationship. I worked on the floor of a busy department store; he worked in the storeroom. On occasion, I helped with deliveries, so I got to know Philip well. He was wise beyond his years and very inspirational.

The summer after I left the job, I heard he had jumped off a 300ft bridge popular for suicides. Fate had it that he landed in a large Arborvitae tree that cushioned his fall. He was very hurt, with broken bones and wounds, but he survived.

I remember the day I heard about it. I was in town doing some shopping when an old work colleague approached me.

"Did you hear about Philip?" she asked. She scanned my face for a reaction. I continued to browse, expecting he had done something embarrassing.

"What about Philip?" I replied, remembering seeing him a couple of days previous but not having the time to stop for a chat.

"You didn't hear? He almost killed himself last night. On life support." I stared at her in disbelief.

"Are you serious? How do you know?" I demanded, refusing to believe it was true. As she filled me in on what happened, I couldn't process it.

When I saw him last, he looked as if he hadn't a care in the world. Everyone thought the world of him, as he was always more than helpful. Whether he knew it or not, Philip had helped me with his advice. I was sad, distraught, and more than anything else, confused. I didn't understand how nobody saw the pain he was feeling.

I didn't understand how someone with such a bright future could attempt to cut it so short. I didn't understand what thoughts could be so dark. What pain could be so deep to lead an intelligent 18-year-old young man to stand on a bridge and decide to jump? I still don't, and I'm not sure if I ever will.

What I did begin to understand was that everyone is going through personal battles they keep to themselves. Sure, smiling at another person as you pass them in a rush or waving when you see someone is a great start. But it's just not enough.

The truth is three simple words have the potential to save a life: "How are you?"

Those three short words let people know you care; you care about how they're feeling. And that might make a difference, the difference between life and death.

So many people cared about Philip, but he didn't know it. If I learned anything from his actions, it's that life moves quickly, and it's so easy to get wrapped up in your own life.

It's easy to miss what's going on around you, in your office, in your classroom, at the same table during a family meal.

It's important to slow down and care enough to ask a question that could make a world of a difference to someone who feels alone, isolated or in pain.

"How are you?" Let the people in your life know you care by giving them a window to open up to you.

Philippians 2:4
Do not merely look out for your own personal interests, but also for the interests of others.

Thankfully, Philip made a full recovery, and now works at a foundation that helps young people with depression and anxiety.

Be A Healer

Our words have the power to heal people. Our words have the ability to lift people out of depression, to help them get through a challenge, giving them the faith they need.

When you tell someone, "I believe in you. I think you're amazing. You will achieve great things," they're not just words of encouragement; they're healing words.

We don't know what people are going through, the pressures they face, or what's going on in their minds. They might seem happy on the outside, have a beautiful house, a loving family, and children you would be proud to have. But on the inside, they could be depressed, discouraged, or stressed over something that happened years ago.

Many people have wounds from the past. Maybe they were bullied or have regrets that replay in their mind. Or, they were told as a child they were useless. Now, no matter what level of success they acquire, they can't shake off that negativity.

Proverbs 12:25
Anxiety in a man's heart weighs it down, But a good word makes it glad.

A few words of encouragement like, I believe in you, you have a beautiful home, a beautiful family, is all that is needed. These words don't take much effort to say, but to them, it can be the healing words they need to hear. It can lift them up into faith by focusing them on the good in their lives.

A few words can lift a person's spirit, making them believe in themselves. Your words can be what keeps them moving forward.

Everywhere I go, I speak to people, when I'm getting a coffee, my morning paper, waiting in line at my local mall. I believe God puts people in our lives on purpose, so we can bring healing. A smile and a few words can change a person's day. Take a moment to bless people with your words.

You have no idea what they have been through or are going through. A few words could break them out of their negative thinking. The thought that someone cares can make all the difference.

Luke 6:31
Do to others, as you would have them do to you.

We all want compliments, encouragement, and to be inspired, so that is what you must give to others. Do this and you will find it is returned 10-fold.

Spark Of Hope

A few weeks ago, waiting for a coffee, I noticed a young lady wearing a suit. I complimented her on how professional she looked. She said thanks but looked back into her phone.

Then the other day, while reading a book and having a coffee, the same young lady approached me. She was very emotional, so I told her to sit down.

She went on to explain that my words had helped her. As she had slept in, she forgot to put on her makeup and was thinking about not attending an important meeting.

She said my words had broken the negative loop that was replaying in her head. She attended the presentation and excelled.

When you feel like complimenting someone, do it without hesitation. The person could be looking very professional, have a warm personality, or a jacket that caught your attention. God didn't put that thought in your head if the other person didn't need it.

You may not know them; it may not make sense to you, but God knows what He is doing. There is a reason they need your compliment. If that young lady had not thanked me, I would never have known the impact of my words.

That's the way you need to see your compliments, your kind words, your encouragement, as the healing words, people need to hear. Don't tell yourself it won't make that much difference.

Be free with words of encouragement and motivation. You never know what is going on with a person. They could look happy, but on the inside, they could be lonely and depressed or even suicidal.

What I have learned is, even those that seem to have it all, success, beautiful house, lovely family, can be lacking something. Often, these are the people that need healing words the most, as everyone expects all is well with them.

Most people would have assumed the young lady had a great job and had a carefree life. Don't let outward appearances keep you from making a compliment.

We don't understand the power a few words of encouragement, motivation, or inspiration can have on a person's life. I believe in you. I know you have what it takes. I am always here if you need me.

Your words may seem ordinary to you, but when they land on ears that need healing energy, they can have a massive impact.

Someone today needs your healing words. They may not get over depression without you letting them know they have value, you care, and there are good things in their future.

They might give up on a dream or talk themselves out of going to an important meeting unless you step up and encourage them.

Will you be a healer? Will you be a motivator? Will you use your words to inspire people?

Proverb 15:4
Gentle words bring life and health.

Philosophy Of A Healer

Many people think, to do God's work, they have to be someone special; they have to pass specific tests. No. To do God's work, you need to think of others before yourself.

You have the power to heal people with your words. You can encourage them, motivate them, and enlighten them. Letting people know you care does more than you can imagine.

When I was younger, I would smile at people, and they would smile back. My thought was, for that moment, I brought happiness to their life. That has been my philosophy for as long as I can remember. I always knew I had the gift of happiness, and it was something I needed to share.

We live in a society filled with negativity on TV, the Internet, and social media. It's now accepted to be disrespectful. People think nothing of running someone down, saying hurtful and critical remarks.

It's been many years since I was at school, but I remember it was a form of comedy to make fun of others and spread gossip. Now, with social media, I can imagine it's ten times worse.

Adults and children need healing words more than ever. Words that encourage, words that inspire, words that motivate.

You have the power to turn someone's life around. You have the power to make people believe in their dreams. You have the power to transform depression into joy, sadness into happiness, fear into faith. And you don't need some unique skill; it won't take you a year to learn. You can do it today.

Without your words of encouragement, without your compliments, certain people may never reach the levels that are possible for them. They may never make the changes that are necessary to achieve what they are destined to achieve.

Take time to be a healer. Bless others with your words.

Philippians 2:13

For it is God who works in you to will and to act in order to fulfill his good purpose.

God needs to work through you to inspire those that may have cast Him to one side. He is counting on you to heal the people in your life. Don't be so caught up in your own life that you pass these opportunities.

If you see someone getting bullied, don't sit back and watch, hoping it will be ok. Make the person know that what the bully is saying or doing is wrong. Tell them they must deal with the situation before it gets out of control.

When you go out of your way to encourage your friend that is down, make the time to see a relative that is sick, stand up for a co-worker, you will be rewarded.

Because you are taking time to think and care for others, God will take time to think and care for you, inspiring you, motivating you, helping you on your way. People need what you have. Your wisdom, your knowledge, your faithful view of life. So be free with your compliments. Don't keep them to yourself.

Your thoughts don't bless anybody, you can think well of your friend all day long but if you never tell them they will never know.

People need your healing words.

Proverbs 16:24
Pleasant words are a honeycomb, Sweet to the soul and healing to the bones.

Imprinted Dream

As a student, I shared a house in my third year. Jamie, one of my housemates, had a friend named Gareth. When I first met him, I complimented him on his style.

When he visited, we would talk about our passion for music. Gareth not only had a great love for music but was an excellent musician. He could play the guitar and bass and was a good singer.

Later that year, his life started to fall apart due to family problems. As there was an empty room at our house, we asked him to move in. Whenever I would hear him play or sing, I would tell him how good he was. I noticed, the more I complimented him, the more he practiced. After university, we all went our separate ways.

Years later, Gareth contacted me through a friend, thanking me for all the encouraging words, for being more of a brother than a friend.

To me, the compliments meant nothing, as I was always impressed with his ability as a musician. But to him, they were the words he needed to hear to carry on. My dream of being a musician had imprinted on him and inspired him to study as a sound engineer. Now, he helps others fulfill their musical visions.

Your friend might be a good musician, a good hairdresser, a good decorator, but if you never tell them, they may never know. You might think, I don't have to tell them; they already know— I told them last week.

What I have found is, you may be the only person that compliments them. So whenever the thought comes up, tell them again. You don't know what they are going through, the battles they are fighting.

It's so refreshing to hear encouraging words; they push us on.

1 Thessalonians 5:11
Therefore encourage one another and build each other up, just as in fact you are doing.

Today, it's easier than ever with social media to let them know you care. "Yeah, just want to say hello, and I hope all is going well for you." It's important to remember your words have healing power.

When someone is ill, and you encourage them, you take the time to reassure them there will be brighter days ahead. Those words contain healing. That person could have given up all hope, but your words spark their faith. Your words made them head out that day, rather than sit indoors feeling sorry for themselves.

It's amazing what a few kind words can do. We don't think anything about it, but to the other person, it breathes life into their spirit.

Sam the Man

In my late teens, a young man joined my running club. Sam was a loner, who never talked much, even when spoken to, and when out on runs, he would stay at the back of the group.

Most people just ignored him, but being a compassionate and empathic person, I reached out to him, making him feel part of the club.

When he would attend, I would make it a point to go over to him and ask him how his running was going. He never said anything, just started a strange combination of stretches. So I would follow his routine.

This type of friendship went on for a couple of years 2-3 times a week.

Well, I went off to university, and I hadn't seen Sam for over 20 years. One Sunday, I met him at church. I asked myself, where do I know this guy from? He introduced himself, "Well, I'm Sam. We used to run together." That's the most I had ever heard him speak.

He went on to tell me that his parents split up when he was very young, meaning he lived on his own from 17. He never felt accepted or loved by anyone. He told me the main reason he attended the running club was to hear me ask how he was and how his running was going because no one else in his life was interested in anything he did.

I didn't know it at the time, but Sam needed my healing words. Those one-sided conversations, letting him know I cared, were like food for his soul. Today, Sam is happily married and a seasoned runner. Today, Sam is a different man.

A few words letting someone know you care might not mean much to you, but they can mean so much to others. They can bring life and health.

Make time for the Sam's in your life, those people that sit quietly on the side lines. Make them feel like someone cares. It doesn't have to be something big, just a simple, how are you today? I believe in you. I know you will fulfill your dreams.

Let them know you care.

Taming the Tongue

It's hard not to mention words that cause wounds when talking about healing words. Words can leave scars; words can tear people apart. Words can make people feel inferior and insecure.

Some people are not reaching their full potential because of hurtful words. They heard someone say, over and over, you can't do anything right, you're a disappointment, you'll never change.

David said in Psalms 64, God protect me from the sharp tongues that the people yield as swords. David refers to hurtful words as swords.

Are you building people up with your words, healing their lives, or are you cutting them down? Are you encouraging them, making them stronger, more inspired, more confident, or are you leaving them wounded or scarred?

We have a responsibility to speak healing words of faith, encouragement, and confidence over the people closest to us. Yes, we have to lead them by example but don't do it in an angry, disrespectful way.

Words said in anger can damage a person's self-image. Never say, "You're useless, you'll never do that. You'll never change." Don't affect others with negativity.

Be a person that educates and motivates and pushes others into their destiny, helping them release their dreams. Be the person people feel they can approach if they do something wrong.

James 3:2-10

For we all stumble in many ways. If anyone does not stumble in what he says, he is a perfect man, able to bridle the whole body as well.

Now if we put the bits into the horses' mouths so that they will obey us, we direct their entire body as well. Look at the ships also, though they are so great and are driven by strong winds, are still directed by a very small rudder wherever the inclination of the pilot desires.

So also the tongue is a small part of the body, and yet it boasts of great things. See how great a forest is set aflame by such a small fire!

And the tongue is a fire, the very world of iniquity; the tongue is set among our members as that which defiles the entire body, and sets on fire the course of our life, and is set on fire by hell.

For every species of beasts and birds, of reptiles and creatures of the sea, is tamed and has been tamed by the human race.

But no one can tame the tongue; it is a restless evil and full of deadly poison. With it we bless our Lord and Father, and with it we curse men, who have been made in the likeness of God; from the same mouth come both blessing and cursing. My brethren, these things ought not to be this way.

Step Into Peace

In our day-to-day lives, we all have conflicts, things we don't like. I'm not saying you will never disagree, never have any tension, never have any stress.

I'm saying, in the heat of the moment, step back and don't make hurtful comments. That's what damages relationships.

Be careful of the words you speak. Yesterday's healing words can be easily wiped out by a few lazy, condescending words said in the heat of the moment.

Controlling your tongue means you don't say everything you feel. It may come up in your mind, you might be right, but have the discipline to keep it to yourself.

Romans 12:17-20

Do not repay anyone evil for evil. Be careful to do what is right in the eyes of everyone. If it is possible, as far as it depends on you, live at peace with everyone. Do not take revenge, my dear friends, but leave room for God's wrath, for it is written: "It is mine to avenge; I will repay," says the Lord. On the contrary: "If your enemy is hungry, feed him; if he is thirsty, give him something to drink. In doing this, you will heap burning coals on his head.

Some people will make it their mission in life to pull you into conflict. They see the favor in your life; they know you are going to do great things. Instead of being happy for you, they let jealousy consume their spirit. They will try to tempt you into conflict. Don't take that bait; don't let your emotions get the best of you.

When some people see you are outgrowing them, they will try to pull you down. They might say hurtful and nasty things, so you stay at their level. Your strength reflects their weakness. Move away from these people. Keep them out of your life.

32 Nails

There was a little boy who had a bad temper. No matter how many times he was sent to his room, the temper remained.

Then his dad decided to take a different approach. He gave the little boy a bag of nails and told him that, every time he lost his temper, he had to hammer a nail into the back fence.

The first day, the little boy hammered 32 nails. As the days and weeks went by, the number of nails went down. He soon discovered it was easier to hold his temper than to drive nails into the robust fence.

Finally, the day came when he didn't lose his temper at all. So the little boy reported to the dad of his achievement. His dad suggested he now take out a nail for every day he was able to hold his temper.

When all the nails were gone, his dad took his son by the hand and took him to the fence, saying, "You have done well, but look at all the holes in the fence. The fence will never be the same again."

When we say things in anger, they can leave a scar just like these holes. And no matter how many times you say sorry, the scar will remain.

Like the little boy, it's so easy to say hurtful words when we are angry or annoyed. We can feel we have a right to say what we do. In my experience, your point may be correct, but the manner in which you say it is not.

Proverbs 29:11

A fool always loses his temper, But a wise man holds it back.

If someone annoys me, rather than letting the negativity effect my spirit, I remove myself from the situation, writing down exactly how I feel, letting out all my emotions. Later, I will extract the central message and approach the person in a calm state. Of course, some people will not listen whether you are calm or not. Keep clear of these people.

Gathering Feathers

A woman repeated some gossip about a neighbor. Within a few days, everyone in the village knew the story, which by that point had been distorted. The neighbor was deeply hurt, not only by the untruths but also by the betrayal of a friend.

The woman who had first passed on the gossip was also wounded, wrecked with guilt over the pain she had caused her friend. She approached her grandfather, a very wise man, to ask what she could do to set things right.

Her grandfather told her, "Go home, get one of your feather pillows, take it outside and empty it out in the lane behind your house. When you have done this, come back and see me."

The woman was confused but followed his advice. Returning, her grandfather told her, "Now I want you to go and collect all the feathers and bring them to me." "But that's impossible," she said. "They'll have blown away."

"Exactly," said her grandfather, "it's easy to scatter them, but it's impossible to get them back. It's the same with gossip. It takes seconds to spread a rumor, but once you do, you can never undo the hurt."

Psalm 141:3

Set a guard, O LORD, over my mouth; Keep watch over the door of my lips.

Claim Your Inheritance

Galatians 4:1

Think of it this way. If a father dies and leaves an inheritance for his young children, those children are not much better off than slaves until they grow up, even though they actually own everything their father had.

If you feel you must always say what's on your mind, no matter who it hurts or who it offends, then you will never grow up. In the eyes of God, you will remain young children. Your inheritance of joy, peace, success, and happiness will never be yours.

Refraining from speaking our minds is much more than just being disciplined. It's about growing up. It's about knowing that, by doing so, our inheritance will be released. I know people in their 50s that still act like children; they haven't learnt to control their mouth.

They still start arguments, still spread gossip, slander and lies.

God does not ask much of us; He simply asks us to be silent if we have nothing positive to say. He asks that we use our words to encourage not to hurt; we use our words to build people up, rather than tear them down.

Next time you're about to say something harsh or harmful in the heat of the moment, ask yourself. "Is this going to build this person up or tear this person down? Is it going to heal or create a wound?"

As you begin to grow up by making the right decisions, God will start to release your inheritance. You will start to see more blessings than you thought possible. You can't speak hurtful words and live a healthy, prosperous, stress-free life.

God hears everything we say. He listens when we speak healing words. He listens when we say hurtful words. He hears when we compliment, encourage, and push others forward and when we are harsh and disrespectful.

Proverbs 13:2
From the fruit of their lips people enjoy good things.

This means, if you sow disrespect, you will reap disrespect. If you sow judgment, pain, or heartache, you will reap those things. But when you sow kindness, compliments, encouragement, mercy, then those things will come back to you.

Spark To Flame

In the writing of this book, I was finding it hard to find a topic. Usually, an idea comes fully formed, and it's a matter of writing it, but this time was different.

Then my brother sent me a text, letting me know how much one of my books had helped him, advising me that if my words were helping him, they were helping hundreds more.

He ended saying, I believe God works through you to heal others. I got very emotional, as that has been my prayer for over 30 years. It's amazing how a few sentences can give you such a lift. When I read those words, I felt a lifting in my spirit.

I felt a new energy, a new joy. I went from feeling stuck, unmotivated— to feeling excited, passionate, flooded with ideas. Creativity was sparked from a few kind words.

James 3:5

A tiny spark can set a great forest on fire.

I'm asking you to start good fires. Ignite people's hopes. Ignite people's dreams. Ignite the flames of passion in their soul. Your words have the ability to lift people up, breathing new life into their spirit.

Be a healer, be an encourager, be a motivator. Speak healing words of faith.

When you feel tempted to say condescending, hurtful, argumentative words, be disciplined enough to let it go. Learn to tame your tongue.

Don't go through life poisoning people with hurtful words. Instead, go through life building people up with healing, encouraging words.

If you do this, you will enjoy your life more; you will have better relationships, a stronger marriage, children that love and respect you.

You will receive your inheritance and live the life that was destined for you.

Be The Change

Johnny grew up on the streets. His parents, due to work and socializing, never had time for him. Having no guidance, Johnny and his friends started to get into more and more trouble for fun.

A neighbor, who always liked Johnny, could see what his future had in store. The caring little boy with so much potential was beginning to change. Old Ben, as he was known, called Johnny over one day. "I was wondering if you could do a little job for me. Can you help me clean my roof guttering, please?"

He held the ladder for Johnny and instructed him how to do the job. Old Ben hadn't much money, but he always praised Johnny for his excellent work.

Before long, Johnny would come over without being asked, as it was the only time he got any praise or encouragement outside of school.

Some neighbors, seeing the excellent job Johnny was doing, asked if he could clean their roof guttering. So, with the help of Old Ben, they cleaned most of the houses on the street, charging £3, which they split. Within a few years, Johnny and Old Ben were doing a few of the nearby streets on the weekends.

When it came to the end of secondary school, Johnny knew what he wanted to do. Now, Johnny runs a successful business, employing a few of his friends. One old man's encouragement changed a young man's life.

Like Johnny, everyone needs encouragement; everyone needs praise, someone that sees the best in them, someone that says, good job, well done, I appreciate that, thanks for your time.

You can be that person. You can be the one that gives praise, the one that doesn't find fault, the one people turn to when they need healing, comforting words. Use words that uplift, not tear down, words that encourage, rather than upset.

If there are no compliments in your home, no praise, no encouragement, it will affect your children. Maybe like Johnny, they will run with the wrong crowd.

Every time Johnny went to help Old Ben, it lifted him; it gave him a sense of worth. We all have that ability. It doesn't take much, a few words to let them know someone cares.

Compliment your husband or wife, child or friend. Tell them you love them, you're proud of them, you're happy they're in your life. Compliments are the glue that holds relationships together.

We all have enough people trying to push us down. Magazines telling us we need to lose weight, wear better clothes, or have the latest car. We all go through moments of self-doubt. We don't think we're good enough to do something, even though we have done it a thousand times before. Negativity even gets to those that have the strongest of faith.

When you become the healing voice for the people in your life, it will lift and inspire you. As you will see the effect your words have on them.

It's so easy to make a compliment, so easy in fact people don't bother, thinking it won't make a difference. Try it today and see the powerful effect it has. Use your words to build people up, telling them what they can become, making them feel better about themselves.

Words That Lift

A group of frogs was hopping through the woods when two of them fell into a bottomless pit. All the other frogs gathered around to see if there was anything they could do.

But when they saw how deep the hole was, they all agreed it was hopeless and decided to tell the two frogs of their fate because there was no way out. Meanwhile, the two frogs in the pit began to jump with all their might.

The group of frogs, looking down at them, shouted into the hole, “It’s hopeless, give up; this is what you get for leaving the group.” But the two frogs continued jumping as hard as they could.

Finally, one of the frogs listened to his friends above. “It's hopeless, give up,” so he resolved himself to his fate, lying down and dying as the others looked on. The other frog persevered, jumping with every ounce of energy he had, although he was exhausted.

His companions yelled louder for him to accept his fate, but the louder they shouted, the harder the weary frog jumped. Finally, he leapt so high that he sprang from the pit.

Amazed, the other frogs celebrated his miraculous achievement. Then asked, "Why did you continue jumping when we told you it was impossible?"

Reading their lips, the shocked frog explained he was deaf. He had perceived their gestures and shouting, as encouragement. They inspired him to try harder.

This simple story contains a powerful lesson. Your encouraging words can lift people up and help them through the day. Your disheartening words can cause people to stop believing and give up.

Your words can even diminish someone in the eyes of others, destroying their influence, and can have a lasting impact on the way others view them. Be careful of what you say.

Speak faith-filled words to everyone in your life.

A Flair For Hair

My mother always wanted to be a hairdresser. She had a deep passion for it, cutting the hair of people in the local community. Everyone told her it was just a dream; there was no money in it.

On leaving school, she was offered a job at the local factory. It was a good paying job with a lot of benefits. Everyone told her it would be mad not to go for it.

A few days later, a relative of one of her regular clients flew in from London. When she saw the haircut my mother did for her friend, she was full of praise and asked her to style her hair.

The woman was delighted with the result, telling her that a similar standard of cut in London would cost 4-5 times what she was charging. Going on, she said she would make an excellent hairdresser and with her skill would be running her own business within years.

Until that point, my mother hadn't heard anything good about hairdressing. In fact, she was starting to think it was just a dream.

But when she heard those words from a complete stranger, it changed her whole attitude. It cleared all the doubtful thoughts from her mind. Not only did my mother think she could be a hairdresser, but she believed she had what it took to open her own business. The negative comments about it just being a dream didn't affect her after that. And, she went on to be a hairdresser.

That was over 40 years ago, and my mother remembers that as if it were yesterday. One compliment can have an impact for a lifetime.

But what if that woman had just thought it and not said it. What if she had talked herself out of it? My mother would never have fulfilled her dream, and she would not have opened and run her own business for 32 years.

Don't withhold your compliments; they can be what make a person step up into their destiny.

Jesus' Secret

Hebrews 4:15

For we do not have a high priest who is unable to empathize with our weaknesses, but we have one who has been tempted in every way, just as we are—yet he did not sin.

Jesus was no different than you or me. Yet, he was able to heal people with a few words and laying of hands. He was able to calm storms and feed 5000 with just five loaves and two fishes. It's easy to say, of course, He could; He was the Son of God, and you would be right. But that was not the only reason.

Jesus spent a lot of time in solitude. It's how he made important decisions. It's how he dealt with the constant demands of his ministry. It's how he taught his disciples.

Mark 1:35-37
Very early in the morning, while it was still dark, Jesus got up, left the house and went off to a solitary place, where he prayed. Simon and his companions went to look for him, and when they found him, they exclaimed: "Everyone is looking for you!"

Jesus knew the most powerful and healing words come from God. Often, He spent the whole night in prayer, talking with his Father, sharing all that was troubling him, listening to ideas that came to him.

Mark 6:31–32
"Then, because so many people were coming and going that they did not even have a chance to eat, he said to them, 'Come with me by yourselves to a quiet place and get some rest.' So they went away by themselves in a boat to a solitary place"

Jesus even invited His disciples to share times of group solitude with Him. Solitude is a spiritual discipline. "Alone time" with God calms the mind. It can be a time of knowing God more deeply, a time of strengthening, a time of refreshment, a time of sharing our deepest concerns.

In today's society, we have distractions 24/7. With work, bills, children, family and social media, we rarely have a moment to ourselves. Is it any wonder we get stressed, depressed, and frustrated?

Regular times of solitude allow us to refocus on what is important, giving us a clear reflection of who we are, and what we need to do, which often means facing up to our weaknesses.

It is good, now and then, to "detach". We need time spent away from others, away from cell phones, away from television, away from social media.

The Bible certainly supports the value of solitude. Psalm 46:10 says, "Be still, and know that I am God." Jesus' closeness with God was the secret of his wisdom, compassion, and power. This power reflected in His words, giving them the ability to heal, to motivate and inspire all whom He met.

Luke 2:52
Jesus grew in wisdom and stature, and in favor with God and man.

Of course, we won't reach Jesus' level of perfect holiness, but little-by-little, we can have a deeper connection to God. Stress, depression, anger, frustration will fade away. There will be a healing within your spirit.

Matthew 4:4
Jesus answered, "It is written: 'Man shall not live on bread alone, but on every word that comes from the mouth of God.

New Perspective

A small boy came to the scene of an accident. The police had cordoned off the road and a bridge, where a truck travelling at high speed had got stuck. The driver had dismissed height restrictions.

The traffic had been redirected, while several tow trucks were trying to pull out the truck. The little boy asked one of the policemen what had happened.

So the policeman explained that the truck had gotten stuck, and they were trying to get it out, but were unable to do so, no matter how many tow trucks came, as the truck was so solidly jammed.

The little boy looked past the crowd, then looked up at him and said, "Why don't they let the air out of the tires." The policeman looked down at him then back at all the grown men trying to pull the truck out from under the bridge and shook his head. And that's what he instructed the men to do, and the truck just rolled out.

The little boy was able to see the problem from a new perspective, and every one of us has that capability. Regular use of solitude calms the mind and allows us to see our problems in a different way.

God is the reason for all creativity, all intuition, and all flashes of insight. He is the source of inspiration and motivation and the ability to see things in a new way.

If my words inspire you, it's not me; it's God inspiring you through my words. I am merely the instrument He uses.

God's energy is available to each one of us, like a power source we can plug into simply by finding the plug. We all have several appointments we must attend. Take the time to have an appointment with yourself this week.

Our heavenly father does not communicate with us when we are mulling over our problems or when we are stressed, worried, doubtful, or depressed. He is only available when we are relaxed, calm, or in prayer. So, it is a good idea to relax and switch off from the world as often as you can.

Luke 5:16

Jesus often withdrew to lonely places and prayed.

Preparing For Solitude

Bring to your solitude whatever will help you to be with Jesus in a personal, interactive way. Your Bible, journal, and pen. If you plan to be outside, you may need appropriate clothes, shoes, chair, or blanket.

Plan to set aside a time and space so you won't be interrupted. Turn off cell phones, laptops etc. Plan a time when family members or others will not disturb you. It might even be an idea to seek out a secluded place or quiet room.

In solitude, everyone struggles with distracting thoughts — don't feel bad about it. When your mind wanders, replace it with a prayer. It may help you to repeat a phrase from the Bible, possibly breathing the words in and out as a Breath Prayer.

Perfect solitude is doing nothing for at least thirty minutes. This can be very challenging at first, so build up. Ten minutes is an excellent place to start. Also, I find that a walk in a quiet forest or on a remote beach can be as good, free of hurry, worry, and stress.

Whatever may be on your mind or troubling you, release it. You may be worried about your work, stressed over a family relationship, or doubtful that a personal matter will resolve itself. Hand each concern over to God.

Be open to whatever answer He has for you. Trust that, even if it is not the message you want to hear, it is the right one for you. Do not judge what feelings may arise. You might feel encouraged or challenged

The right thing to do is sometimes the hardest.

Acting On Wisdom

It is subtle, and when answers come to you, it is vital you act upon them straight away. If you get the feeling you must contact a relative, don't let stubbornness or pride stop you from making the call.

It's not as if we do not have the same connection to God as Jesus did; it's the fact that Jesus asked for answers, and when He received them, He acted without question.

What most people do when the correct idea comes into their head is to talk themselves out of it, convince themselves that making up with a neighbor or co-worker wouldn't make that much difference anyway.

They dismiss God’s word and deal with the consequences, more stress heartache and pain.

Proverbs 3:6 (MSG)
Listen for God's voice in everything you do, everywhere you go; he's the one who will keep you on track.

From my experience, the more you listen and act on moments of insight, the deeper your connection with God becomes.

Release The Healing

There are people in your life right now that need your healing. They need your blessing; they need your encouragement. You can be the one that helps them to fulfill their destiny. You can be the one that saves a life by breaking the chains of depression. You can be the one that ignites a persons faith.

Look around this week with the attitude, "Who can I bless, who can I encourage, who can I push into their destiny."

If you develop the habit of speaking healing words in your life, those seeds are going to come back to you. God is going to cause you to rise higher, go further, and achieve more than you ever thought possible. You will accomplish dreams, overcome obstacles, and become everything God created you to be.

Be the healing voice that every one needs to hear.

ABOUT THE AUTHOR

I live on the northwest coast of Ireland. I use this medium to share my true voice. I wish to enlighten others and help them to see that God wants the very best for them. We often make it hard for him to enter our lives as we focus on the dark clouds rather than the silver lining.

In this growing digital frontier I just want to shed a little light out into the world to light up peoples lives in the hope that they to will help inspire others which will slowly but surely change the world, even in a small way.

My Other Books

Gods Perfect Timing
The Power Of Letting Go
The Power Of Choice
The Power Of Words
The Power of Faith Can Move Mountains
Make Space for God

Printed in Poland
by Amazon Fulfillment
Poland Sp. z o.o., Wrocław

61232054R00040